7/97 (21)

1/06 ✓ (3)

P9-AGD-231

The Young Scientist Investigates

Food

by
Terry Jennings

CHILDRENS PRESS®
CHICAGO

Illustrated by
Joy Barling Loyla
Wendy Brett
Peter Kesteven
Edward McLachlan
Mike Saunders

Library of Congress Cataloging-in-Publication Data

Jennings, Terry J.
    Food / by Terry Jennings.
      p.   cm. — (The Young scientist investigates.)
    Includes index.
    Summary: An introduction to food and nutrition with
accompanying study questions, activities, and experiments.
    ISBN 0-516-08402-X
    1. Food—Juvenile literature. 2. Nutrition—Juvenile literature.
3. Food—Experiments—Juvenile literature. [1. Food
2. Nutrition.] I. Title. II. Series: Jennings, Terry J. Young
scientist investigates.
    TX355.J46   1988
    641.3—dc 19   88-22866
                                    CIP
                                    AC

North American edition published in 1989 by Regensteiner
Publishing Enterprises, Inc.

© Terry Jennings 1984
First published 1984 by Oxford University Press

Printed in the United States of America
1 2 3 4 5 6 7 8 9 10 R 98 97 96 95 94 93 92 91 90 89

The Young Scientist Investigates
Food

Contents

Food

Eating is fun, especially when you are hungry. Most people have a favorite food. Some people enjoy eating sweet things like cakes, chocolates, and ice cream. Other people enjoy savory foods like cheese and meat. Enjoying eating is our body's way of making sure that it gets the things it needs to work properly.

Food helps us to keep warm. It also gives us the energy to walk, talk, run, and do all the other things we do. Food helps us to grow. It also helps us to stay healthy.

Some of our foods come from animals. Some come from plants. Many of our foods, like bread, cheese, and meat are solids. A few, like milk and soup, are liquids. Some of our food is grown in this country. Some come from other countries.

Can you think of any other animals that eat grass?

Food chains

Every living thing in the world has to have food to live. A small animal, such as a fly, needs very little food. But a large animal like an elephant has to eat a lot of food every day.

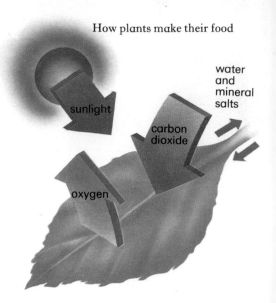

How plants make their food

Unlike animals, plants can make their own food. A green plant can use the sun's energy to make its own food. It uses the sun's energy to turn carbon dioxide gas from the air, and water and mineral salts from the soil, into food.

Animals cannot make their own food. Many animals have to eat plants. Cows, sheep, rabbits, deer, horses, and goats are just some of the animals that feed on plants. Some animals eat plant-eating animals. So all animal food comes directly or indirectly from plants.

We humans eat vegetables like potatoes, carrots, cabbages, peas, beans, fruits, and nuts of all kinds. These have come from plants. We also eat meat, eggs, and cheese or drink milk. These things have come from animals of various kinds that feed on plants. The fish we eat feed either on plants or on small animals, which themselves eat plants.

The way in which animals and plants are linked together by their food is called a food chain. All food chains begin with plants. Here is a simple food chain.

Energy

Filling a car with gas

In what ways are these children using energy?

In the picture opposite we can see cars being driven along a road. One car is being filled up with gas at a gas station. A car can move about and carry people and their belongings. In order to do these things the car must have energy. The car gets its energy from the gas. The energy is set free when the gas is burned inside the engine. The heat that is made from the engine warms the car's passengers. A car engine gets all its energy for movement, working, carrying things, and warmth, from its fuel. The car's fuel is gas.

Just like engines, we must all have a fuel to give us the energy we need to move, to work, to play, and even to talk. We also use some of this energy to keep our bodies warm. We must give our bodies the right kind of fuel. This is food. In our bodies the food is slowly burned. This burning is much too slow a process to produce flames and smoke. But it does produce warmth and the energy for doing things.

Energy-giving foods

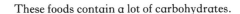

These foods contain a lot of carbohydrates.

Inside our bodies food is burned. Scientists call the foods that give our bodies energy, carbohydrates and fats. Most of the carbohydrates we eat come from plants. These carbohydrates are mainly starch and sugar. Bread, cakes, jam, and potatoes contain a lot of carbohydrates. Plants make these carbohydrates, using the energy of the sun. The picture shows some foods that contain a lot of carbohydrates. Carbohydrates are foods that give us plenty of energy.

Fats give us even more energy. Some fats come from animals, some from plants. Butter, margarine, lard, and cooking oil are fats. The fatty parts of meat and bacon also contain fats, and there is some fat in milk and peanuts. Fried foods contain a lot of fat. Some foods rich in fats are shown in the picture.

These foods contain a lot of fat.

The body can make its own fats. It does this when we eat more food than we really need. Then our body stores this extra food as fat. Some of this fat is useful because it helps to keep us warm. Some of it can give us energy if we have not eaten for a long time. But too much fat in our bodies may be harmful. The heart has to do extra work to allow us to carry this fat around.

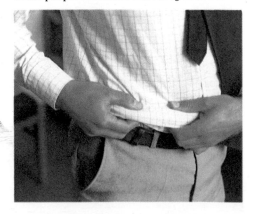

Some people are fatter than they need be.

Body-building foods

If a car is damaged or broken down, someone at the garage repairs it. If any parts of the car are broken or missing, the mechanic can get new ones and fix them. Sometimes our bodies are damaged. We cut ourselves and sometimes we break bones. Parts of our body are also wearing out. We are, for example, all the time rubbing away the outer layers of our skin. A car cannot repair itself, but we can. New parts can grow inside us. The material for the repair of our bodies comes from part of our food. The part of the food is called protein.

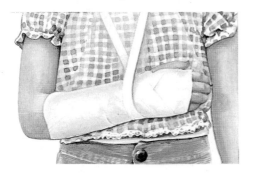

Unlike a car, we can grow as well as repair ourselves. Protein-rich food allows us to grow. A growing boy or girl needs a lot of protein for bodybuilding. But even a grown-up needs protein to repair damaged parts of the body and to replace parts that are wearing out.

How we grow up

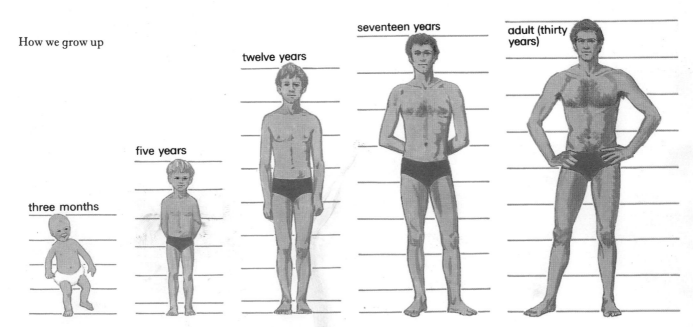

three months

five years

twelve years

seventeen years

adult (thirty years)

Proteins

Proteins are bodybuilding foods. Proteins are found in lean meat, fish, nuts, beans, and peas. Very small babies have to grow quickly. They feed on milk. Milk has protein in it as well as some carbohydrates and fats. Milk also has other things in it which keep us healthy. That is why milk is good for you. Cheese is made from milk and that has a lot of protein too.

Baby being breastfed

Egg white is almost all protein and water. Proteins build your body and repair damaged parts. Proteins make it possible for your muscles and bones to grow. Proteins keep your body strong. They also give you some energy.

It would be bad for us if we ate nothing but proteins. We need some foods of each kind. If we eat several things, we usually get proteins, carbohydrates, and fats. Some bread, for example, is made from wheat. The food in bread is mainly starch, which is a carbohydrate. But there is some protein. When we put butter or margarine on bread, we are adding fat. So if we eat a grilled cheese or peanut butter and jelly sandwich we are getting proteins, carbohydrates and fats. If we eat fish and French fries, we get carbohydrates and some fats from the fries. Then there is a lot of protein and some fats in the fish.

Mineral salts

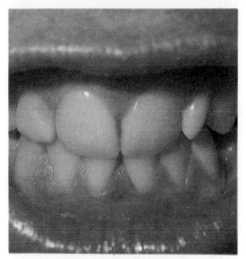

Most foods have some mineral salts in them. Some of these minerals are used, together with proteins, to build our bones. Others are used to help build our muscles and nerves. Still other mineral salts are used for our teeth and blood. Mineral salts are used in all parts of our body. One of the most important minerals is calcium. Calcium is found in milk, butter, cheese, yogurt, bread, cabbage, and many other foods. Calcium is used by your body to make healthy bones and teeth.

Another important mineral is iron. Iron is needed for healthy red blood. But we do not have to eat nails or screws to keep our blood red and healthy! To do this in fact would make us very ill. We need only tiny amounts of iron. Such small amounts of iron are found in foods like liver, corned beef, and sardines. Eggs, bread, and baked beans also contain iron. So do chocolate and dried fruits such as raisins and dates. Eating any of these foods will help our blood to stay red and healthy.

Vitamins

Like mineral salts, vitamins also keep us healthy. But your body uses vitamins only in tiny amounts. Some people buy pills or tablets containing vitamins. But these are not really necessary, because most of us get more than enough vitamins from our food. Vitamins help all parts of the body to work properly and to stay healthy. Some vitamins help keep our eyes and skin healthy. Others make our blood vessels strong.

These foods contain a lot of vitamin C.

Scientists name vitamins after letters of the alphabet. Vitamin C is found in fresh fruit and green vegetables. Oranges, grapefruit, rose hips, lettuce, brussels sprouts, and spinach contain a lot of vitamin C. Vitamin C keeps our skin and gums healthy.

Our bodies make vitamin D in the sun.

You can get all the vitamins you need if you eat the right foods. We are able to make one vitamin, vitamin D, for ourselves if the skin gets enough sunlight. It is good to get plenty of fresh air and sunshine, but we can also get vitamin D if we eat fish, milk, butter, cheese, and margarine. Vitamin D helps our bones to grow strong and hard. Some of the foods that contain a lot of vitamins are shown in the picture.

Do you remember?

(Look for the answers in the part of the book you have just been reading, if you do not know them.)

1 What are four reasons for eating food?

2 Name two foods that are liquids.

3 How do plants make their food?

4 Name four animals that feed on plants.

5 What is a food chain?

6 Write down a food chain beginning with a cabbage plant.

7 How do we get energy from food?

8 Where do carbohydrate foods come from?

9 Name four foods that contain a lot of carbohydrates.

10 Where do fats come from?

11 Name four foods that contain a lot of fats.

12 What do our bodies get from carbohydrates and fats?

13 Why is it harmful to have too much fat in our bodies?

14 Name one part of our body that is wearing away all the time.

15 Why do grown-ups need proteins as well as children?

16 Name four foods that have a lot of protein in them.

17 What kinds of foods would we get from a peanut butter and jelly sandwich?

18 Why do our bodies need calcium?

19 Name three foods that contain a lot of calcium.

20 Why do our bodies need iron?

21 Name three foods that contain a lot of iron.

22 Why do we need vitamins?

23 How can we get vitamin D?

Things to do

1 **Make sets.** Collect pictures of different foods. Make sets of your pictures. You might for a start divide your pictures up into those that come from plants and those that come from animals. Other sets could be foods grown or produced in this country and those that come from other countries, or fresh foods, packaged foods, frozen foods, dried foods, and canned foods.

Make wall charts of your pictures of foods under these different headings.

2 Mealtimes. Draw a large circle on a sheet of paper. Mark on the edge of the circle the numbers 1 to 24. Pretend this is a 24-hour clock. Mark on it the times when you have your meals and snacks. What is the shortest gap between main meals? What is the longest gap between main meals?

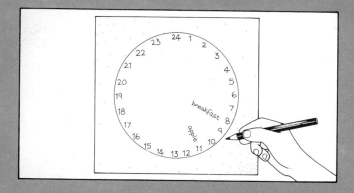

Do you know why we call the first meal of the day "breakfast"? Why is it bad for people not to eat anything at breakfast time?

3 Fruit and vegetable pictures. Make large drawings of small pieces of fruits and vegetables. Some you might draw are a thin slice of cucumber, banana, orange, lemon, onion, tomato, apple, or strawberry. Draw pictures of these fruits or vegetables cut lengthwise or crosswise. Others you might draw include a lettuce leaf, a brussels sprout, or a bean opened out. Paint or color your drawings. Arrange them in a pattern and stick them onto a large sheet of dark-colored paper.

If you can, you might draw some of the pieces of fruits and vegetables onto cloth and embroider them.

4 Fish. Look in your local grocery store and see how many different kinds of fish it sells. What do we mean when we talk about "shellfish"? What are the main places in America where the different kinds of fish and shellfish are caught?

Find out the difference between fresh fish and smoked fish.

Make a list of the kinds of fish sold in cans.

How are fish sticks made?

5 The world is our pantry. Many of the foods we buy in the shops are sold in cans, packets, bottles, or jars. The labels on them should tell us what is inside the container. They also tell us the name of the town or country where the food was grown or packaged.

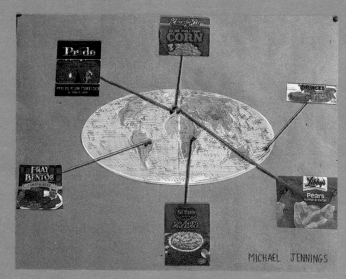

MICHAEL JENNINGS

Obtain a small map of the world and put it in the center of a large sheet of paper or card. Around the edges of the sheet of paper or card, stick the labels or packet fronts of foods that were grown in other countries. For each label put a pin on the map in the country it came from. Then join the label to the pin by a thread. Tape the end of the thread onto the label.

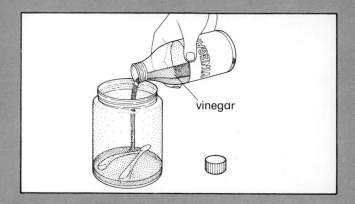

vinegar

6 Vitamin C. Collect pictures of foods that contain a lot of vitamin C. Which of these foods do you eat most often? Which of these foods is sometimes difficult to get in winter?

Every day for a week, keep a record of the foods you eat that have vitamin C in them.

7 Food types. Cut out pictures of foods from magazines. Sort the pictures into groups according to the main food types – bodybuilding, protective, and energy giving. Make wall charts of your pictures.

8 Milk. Do you know the name of the dairy that delivers the milk to your school? Do you know where the dairy is? Where does it get its supply of milk? How is the milk taken to the dairy?

9 Calcium in bones. As we saw on page 9, calcium makes our bones strong and hard. You can see how the calcium works if you soak a small clean bone, such as a chicken bone, in a jar of vinegar for a few days. The vinegar dissolves the calcium in the bone.

Carefully take the bone from the vinegar using a spoon. Wash the bone in cold water. Now feel the bone. What is it like? Can you imagine what your skeleton would be like if all the calcium were taken away from your bones? Your bones would also be like this if you did not eat enough foods containing vitamin D.

10 Baby foods. Have you ever seen a young baby being fed? Some young babies are fed milk from a bottle, some milk from their mother's breast. Why can't a baby eat meals, such as those we eat, right away? How does the baby tell its mother it is hungry?

What do other mammals and birds feed their babies? How long does it take before each kind of baby animal starts to eat the same kinds of foods that adults eat?

11 A poem. Write a poem called "Food, glorious food" to describe the things you like to eat most. If you can, write music to go with your poem. What instruments will you use to make the music?

12 Foods with added vitamins. Many foods, particularly those sold in packets and bottles, contain added or extra vitamins. Read what is written on the labels. Make a list of all the foods that contain added or extra vitamins. Against each food say what vitamins have been added to it.

13 The cost of food. Choose four foods – two produce items and two dairy items. Find out how much they cost in several stores. Check the prices again in the same stores four weeks later. Have the prices gone up or down? Can you find out why the prices of foods change in this way?

14 Vegetarians. Some people will not eat meat at all. This is because they do not like the idea of eating animals. Instead of meat these people eat lots of food plants. Because of this they are called vegetarians. Often vegetarians will eat eggs and cheese and drink milk, even though these foods come from animals.

If you know someone who is a vegetarian, ask him what things he eats instead of meat. Does he eat eggs and cheese, or drink milk? If so, what reason does he give?

15 A new food. Pretend you have discovered a completely new food. It might be a food that has come from a new kind of plant or animal, or it might be a new recipe you have invented.

Draw a picture of your new food. Describe its color, shape, taste, smell, and what it is like to eat. Say why the food is good for you.

Try to make up an advertisement to persuade your friends to buy your new food. Your advertisement might be a poster or it could be a short play. If it is a play make it last 30 or 60 seconds, as those used in television advertisements.

16 Wheat. Wheat is a kind of grain. It is called a cereal because it has a seed, or grain, that we can eat. Many of our breakfast cereals are made from wheat. Some are made from corn or other grains. Find out the names of some breakfast cereals that are made from wheat, oats, rice, and corn. Which part of the wheat plant does flour come from?

Grow some cereal grains in flower pots of soil or seed compost.

17 Food chains. Collect pictures of plants and animals that eat plants and those that eat other animals. Arrange your pictures in food chains. Make a wall chart of your food chains. Write a sentence or two about each one.

18 Quick bread. Ordinary bread, made with yeast, takes a lot of time and patience. Here is a quickly made loaf that uses self-rising flour instead of yeast to make the bread rise. Ask a grown-up to help you with the recipe and with the baking. Wash your hands thoroughly before you begin work.

You need: 2 cups of self-rising flour
1 heaped teaspoon of salt
3 tablespoons of vegetable oil
milk

What you do:

1. Place the flour in a bowl and stir in the salt.

2. Put the vegetable oil in a large measuring cup and add enough milk to fill it up to 1¼ cups.

3. Whisk the oil and milk together and pour them onto the flour and salt. Stir gently until all the flour is moistened. Press the mixture lightly with your fingers. Then turn it onto a floured working surface and knead it with the tips of your fingers until the dough just holds together in a single lump.

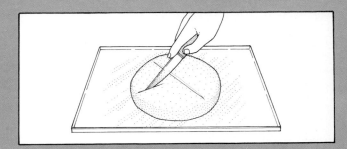

4. Place the dough, smooth side up, on a greased baking tray. Flatten the dough with your knuckles until it forms a thick round. Use a knife to cut a deep cross in the top of the dough.

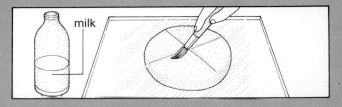

5. Brush the surface of the dough with milk. Then bake it in a hot oven (*careful!*) at 425°F. for 20 to 25 minutes until the loaf is golden brown and feels firm.

Water

Your body needs water as well as solid foods. People have lived for a month or more without food. But no one can stay alive more than a few days without water.

We need water.

A large part of your body is made up of water. About two-thirds of your body is water. You lose water when you go to the bathroom. You also lose water as you breathe and as you sweat. In hot weather you lose even more water because you sweat more. Then you feel very thirsty. If you are to stay healthy, each day you must drink as much water as your body loses.

Water is important in the body because it helps to dissolve or digest many foods. When food is dissolved it can move around your body in the blood. Your blood is mostly water. Water is found in most of the foods you eat and in the milk you drink. All other drinks are mostly water. Many drinks we buy in bottles or cans are just water, sugar, and flavoring. Often these drinks have carbon-dioxide gas in them to make them fizz.

The drinks we buy have a great deal of water.

Digestion

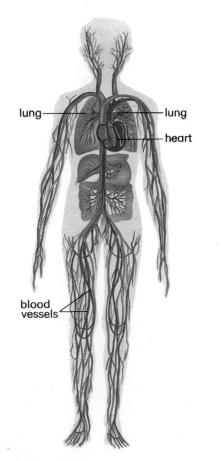

mouth

Esophagus

Liver

Stomach

Pancreas

Large intestine

Small intestine

appendix

anus

Where our food is digested

lung

lung

heart

blood vessels

If the food we eat is to be of any use, it has to get to all parts of our bodies. The food is carried there in the blood. The breaking down of food into bits small enough to be able to pass into the blood is called digestion. Digestion is really making some of the food dissolve.

Digestion goes on in a long tube that runs through your body. This tube has two openings. One opening is the mouth. Here food and drinks enter your body. The other opening is the anus. There unused food leaves the body.

Digestion begins in the mouth. As we chew food with our teeth, a liquid called saliva is mixed with the food. This has a chemical in it that turns some of the food into sugar. In the stomach another chemical begins to dissolve the protein foods. After this the food enters a long coiled tube called the intestines. Here many more chemicals finish the work of dissolving the food. They dissolve the carbohydrates, proteins, and fats. The dissolved foods pass through the walls of the intestines. They go into the blood. The blood takes the dissolved food to all parts of the body.

This diagram shows some of the many blood vessels in the body.

Fiber

Not all food can be digested. The pits of some fruits and the stringy pieces in apples and celery cannot be digested. Nor can parts of other fruits and vegetables. The parts of fruits and vegetables that cannot be digested are called fiber.

Fiber is found in fruit, vegetables, bran cereals, wholewheat bread, and brown rice. Fiber passes right through our bodies without being digested. But fiber is good for us because it helps push the other food through our intestines. Fiber helps carry waste away from the body. If we do not eat enough fiber, we may become constipated. This means we find it very difficult or painful to get rid of the waste food when we go to the bathroom. Food with a lot of fiber in it makes us feel full. That way we do not eat more food than we really need.

These fruits and vegetables contain lots of fiber

These manufactured foods contain lots of fiber

Keeping food fresh

Freshly caught fish is packed in ice.

Mold can grow on food.

Until quite recently most food could not be kept for very long. Most food had to be eaten while it was fresh. This meant that many foods were not available in the winter. And people in big towns could not get much fresh food to eat. If someone had tried to keep these foods, they would have gone bad quickly.

Food goes bad because tiny plants called bacteria and mold grow on it. Bacteria and mold grow on food when it is warm or moist. Bacteria and mold cannot grow on very cold food.

Packing food in ice is one way of keeping food fresh. This is done with fish on trawlers out at sea. Refrigerators and deep freezers are easier ways of keeping food fresh. With refrigerators and freezers we can eat fresh food at any time. We can even eat fresh fruits like strawberries at Christmas, long after they were grown in the field or gardens. We can eat food that has come from countries far away. The food is kept fresh on the long journey in a refrigerator or freezer.

A refrigerator-freezer

Some more ways of keeping food

Bacteria and mold cannot grow without water. People have always preserved some foods by drying. For hundreds of years, fruits and herbs have been dried in the sun. Nowadays we often eat dried fruits like dates, raisins, and prunes. In some countries people dry meat and fish in the sun. Even liquid foods like milk and soup can be dried. Later, when they are wanted, water is added to the powdered milk or soup. Potatoes and peas can be dried. Again water is added to them to make the potatoes and peas swell up to their original shape.

Another way of keeping food is in cans. The fruits, vegetables, or meats are put into open cans. The fruits, vegetables, or meats are boiled to kill off any bacteria and molds. Then the can is sealed so that no bacteria and mold can reach the foods.

Bacteria and mold cannot live in salt or vinegar. Some foods are pickled in salt or vinegar to keep them. Bacteria and mold cannot live in a strong sugar solution. That is why jam will keep. Because of the different ways of keeping food, we can eat food long after it was prepared. Today we can eat food that was picked four or five years ago. We can also bring food to places such as tops of mountains or deserts where nothing grows.

Drying fish in the sun

Jams and preserves

Enjoying food

Most people enjoy the sight, smell, and taste of food, particularly if they are hungry. Our mouth starts to water if we see some food we like. Our mouth may even start to water if we think about some food we like. Our mouth is producing saliva for when we eat.

You taste food with your tongue. Look in a mirror and stick your tongue out. You will see little red bumps on your tongue. These are the taste buds. We have four kinds of taste buds on our tongue. On one part of your tongue you can taste bitter foods. On another you taste salty things. You taste sour foods on another part of your tongue and sweet foods on a different part. Your taste buds send a message to your brain that the food you are eating is bitter, salty, sweet, sour, or a mixture of these flavors.

Taste buds on a human tongue

Most of the food you taste, you really smell too. Often your food does not seem to taste as good when you have a cold. When you have a cold your taste buds carry on working well. But when your nose is stuffed the flavor of the food cannot get to the part of the nose where you smell the food. And so your food does not seem to taste the way it usually does.

Fun foods

If we are to stay healthy and active we need to eat foods that give us proteins, carbohydrates, fats, mineral salts, and vitamins. We also need water and fiber. But sweets often contain only sugars that are carbohydrates. Sweets give us energy, but on their own they do not allow us to grow. Also, too many sweets make teeth decay or rot.

Decayed teeth

Some other snack foods that you can buy have few proteins, vitamins, mineral salts, or fiber. Often, like sweets, these foods have lots of sugar or starch in them. Most of these foods are man-made. Chips, sherbet, cotton candy, pop rocks, and chewing gum are like this. So are popsicles and artificial fruit drinks. Many of these foods taste nice and are fun to eat or drink. But they will not help your body grow and stay healthy. If you eat too much of some of these foods, you may be getting too much sugar. This may make your teeth decay. The sugar or starch may also stop you from feeling hungry. Then you may not feel like eating the other foods you need.

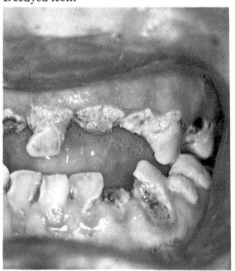

Here are some good snack foods: apples, nuts, celery, and carrots. These will stop you from feeling hungry and do you good. These snack foods also will help you keep your teeth clean.

Some good snack foods

Food and famine

We are lucky because we get enough to eat. We can all eat the right foods. We can also drink clean and fresh water. Some of us eat more than we need and the extra is stored in our bodies, mainly as fat. Our clothes do not fit and our heart has to work harder so that we can carry around the extra weight.

Which meal would you like?

But many people in the world do not get enough food. The farmers in some countries cannot grow food for everyone. Often the people are too poor to be able to buy enough food. Sometimes there is too little rain for crops to grow. And so the people go hungry. When there is no food for the people it is called a famine.

Floods, earthquakes, volcanoes and wars may also destroy the crops. Pests and diseases may kill the crop plants. Then there is famine.

Scientists are trying to find new ways to grow more food. New kinds of plants are being bred which will grow in dry or cold parts of the world. New fertilizers are being made so that the plants will grow better. New chemicals have been made to kill weeds and insect pests. Dams can be built to provide water for crops and people in dry areas. New machines can sow and harvest more crop plants. Unfortunately all of these things cost a lot of money. And not all people in poor countries can buy them.

Making plants grow in the desert

Do you remember?

(Look for the answers in the part of the book you have just been reading if you do not know them.)

1 How much of our body is water?

2 What are three ways in which our body loses water?

3 What is digestion?

4 What liquid is added to food as we chew it?

5 What does this liquid do to the food?

6 What happens to food in the stomach?

7 Where does the digested food go?

8 What part of the food is fiber?

9 Which foods contain a lot of fiber?

10 Why is fiber useful?

11 What are the tiny plants that make food go bad?

12 Why does ice or a refrigerator keep food fresh?

13 Name three foods that can be preserved by drying.

14 What is done to food before it is sealed in cans?

15 What do we use to taste our food?

16 Why does your food not seem to taste as good when you have a cold?

17 Why are too many sweets bad for us?

18 Name four good snack foods.

19 Why do some people not get enough food to eat?

20 How are scientists trying to find new ways to grow more food?

Things to do

1 How much water do you drink every day? To find out how much water you drink every day, get a plastic measuring cup. Start off in the morning and measure any liquid that you drink. Do not forget that milk and fruit juices are mostly water! Remember also to measure any milk you put on your breakfast cereal. Do the same thing with soup, jello, and any other watery foods you eat. Keep this record for all your meals and snacks for a whole day and then add up the total.

About how much water did you take into your body? Work out how much water you drink in a week, a month, and a year. What happens to most of this water?

(As well as the liquids you drink, many foods such as fruits and vegetables also contain water.)

2 Your teeth. Take a bite into an apple. Look at the bite marks in the apple. Which of your teeth did the biting? Now chew a piece of the apple. Which teeth grind the apple into small pieces?

Can you think of one reason why babies only drink milk?

3 How many teeth do you have? Study your own teeth in a mirror. Make a record chart of your teeth like this. Each little square is for one tooth. Grown-ups can have 32 teeth (16 in each jaw). How many do you have?

Fill in your tooth chart like this:
If a tooth is filled put a small black circle like this

If a tooth is missing, put a cross like this

If a tooth is decayed, shade it in like this

How does your tooth chart compare with those of your friends? Who has the most healthy teeth?

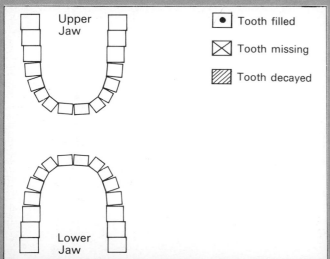

4 Tasting. Take a sugar cube, pinch of salt, a small piece of toast, and a small piece of dark or bitter chocolate.

Wash your hands thoroughly. Then, look in a mirror and see where on your tongue you can taste each one best. Make a drawing of your tongue and mark on it where you tasted each of these four things.

If your friends do this experiment, do they obtain the same results as you did?

5 Tasting and smelling food. Without looking at them or smelling them, can you tell the difference between pieces of onion, apple, celery, carrot, and raw potato?

Wash your hands thoroughly, and then cut these fruits and vegetables into pieces all the same size.

Blindfold a friend. Ask him to hold his nose. Give him one of the pieces and ask him to tell you what it is. Does he guess right? Now try him with each of the other pieces of fruit or vegetable in turn.

Change places with your friend and see if you can do better than he did.

6 Smells. Think of five different foods that have smells you like very much. Look through magazines and find pictures of these five foods. Cut out these pictures and stick them neatly onto a large sheet of paper. Write by the side of each picture why you like the particular smell of each food.

Find out which foods other people in your class most like to smell. Do they like the same smells as you?

7 The long journey. Pretend you are able to change your size so that you can get into a tiny transparent plastic capsule. The capsule is small enough to be swallowed when it is put in someone's food. Write a story describing your adventures as you journey with the food through the digestive system.

8 A model robot. Make a model robot. Give your robot a simple digestive system.

Use a large box for the body and a smaller box for the robot's head. His arms and legs could be made from shampoo bottles or tin cans.

The robot's mouth might be a plastic funnel. Other parts of the digestive system could be made from plastic or rubber tubing and plastic bags. Fix them in place with pieces of thin wire, clay, or glue.

9 A new disease. Imagine there is a new disease called donutitis, which is caused by eating too many donuts. Write a story about a boy or girl who got donutitis. Describe how the boy or girl caught the disease, what happened, and how he or she was finally cured.

10 My favorite foods. Make a book or a wallchart. Give the book or wallchart the heading "My favorite foods." Try to find pictures of the foods or meals you really enjoy. Stick the pictures in your book or on your chart. Write a sentence or two about each of the foods. Say what you like about each food. Think of its taste, its color, its smell and how you feel after you have eaten that food.

11 Old people and food. Do old people eat as much food as other grown-ups? Why? Do they enjoy their food as much as you? Are there any kinds of foods that old people cannot manage to eat now that they used to eat? Why is this?

12 Why do we cook food? Look carefully at cooked and uncooked food. Look at it with a hand lens or magnifying glass. Poke the food with a fork to see how tender it is. Compare the color and smell of the cooked and uncooked food. In the case of fruits and vegetables, such as an apple, potato, cabbage, and carrot you could taste a small piece of the raw and cooked food, but *do not* do this with meat or fish. Make a table of your results like this:

	Cooked or uncooked ?	color	wet or dry	hard or soft	smell	taste	other differences
Apple	cooked uncooked						
Potato	cooked uncooked						
Cabbage	cooked uncooked						

13 Famine. Make a list of the countries where people are suffering from famine or starvation or have suffered in recent years. Use a map to find out where these countries are. Do these countries have hot or cold climates, are they wet or dry for much of the year? Are there any other reasons why people in a country may suddenly not have enough food?

14 Make a charity collection. Organize a charity collection in your school to help raise money for people who do not get enough to eat. Ask your teacher to help you. You might be able to collect tin cans, old newspapers, or used stamps and have a rummage sale or hold a concert to raise money. Find out about organizations such as Oxfam or the Save the Children Fund. See what you can do to help them.

15 Space food. Use books to find out what kinds of foods astronauts eat. How do they store, heat, and eat their food?

16 Make a collage. Make a collage by pasting together small cut-out pictures to make one large interesting picture about food. Perhaps you could remind people that not everyone has enough to eat by including a picture of a starving child.

17 School meals. Carry out a survey among your friends at school. Find out which is the most popular school meal. Which is the least popular meal? Make a block graph of your findings.

18 Irish potato bread. On page 15, we made Quick Bread. Here is a recipe for a completely different kind of bread that looks like a pancake. It is good served hot or cold with butter. It is delicious fried with bacon for breakfast.

Ask a grown-up to help you with the recipe and with the baking. Wash your hands thoroughly before you start work.

You need: 2 cups of potatoes
¼ cup butter or margarine
½ cup of self-rising flour
½ teaspoon of salt

What you do:
1. Peel the potatoes. Cook them in boiling water for 20 minutes (*careful!*), then drain them and mash them until they are smooth. Leave the potatoes until they are cold.
2. Rub the butter or margarine into the flour until the mixture looks like breadcrumbs. Add the salt and mix it in well. Add the potatoes and mix them all together with your hands.
3. Roll out the potato dough on a floured working surface. Roll out the dough until it is only about ⅓ of an inch thick. Cut the dough into squares about 2 inches by 2 inches.
4. Heat an ungreased heavy frying pan (*careful*). Cook the potato bread squares on both sides until they are golden brown.
5. Eat your potato bread while it is still hot with butter spread on it. Or leave it to cool on a folded paper towel.

20 Chewing bread. Put a piece of dry bread into your mouth and notice how it tastes. Now chew the bread for as many times as you can without swallowing it — say 25 times. What do you notice about the taste of the bread? What do you think has happened?

Experiments to try

Do your experiments carefully. Write or draw what you have done and what happens. Say what you have learned. Compare your findings with those of your friends.

1 How much food does a slug or snail eat in a day? It is not easy to carry out experiments on the amount of food eaten by humans, but in this experiment you can see how much food a slug or snail eats.

What you need: A small plastic box or some other similar container; some paper towels; a large slug or snail; a lettuce or cabbage leaf; a piece of graph paper; a pencil.

What you do: Line the box with wet paper towels.

Lay the lettuce leaf or cabbage leaf on the graph paper and carefully draw around it.

Put the leaf in the box and gently put the slug or snail on it. Cover the box with a lid with small breathing holes in it, or with a piece of plastic in which small holes have been pierced. Leave the box in a quiet corner, away from heaters and radiators, for 24 hours.

At the end of 24 hours look at the leaf. Compare the new outline with the old one. Lay the leaf on the graph paper and mark out the pieces that have been eaten. Count how many squares of the leaf the slug or snail has eaten.

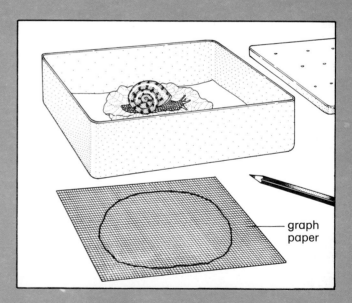

graph paper

Try the experiment again with other kinds of leaves.

Does the slug or snail eat more if it is kept in a cool place or in a warm place? Does it eat more or less if it is kept in total darkness for 24 hours?

2 Testing food for starch. Starch is found in many foods. It also is used for stiffening collars and some dresses after they have been washed. The starch we eat and the starch used in washing clothes came originally from plants. In this experiment we are going to find out which foods contain starch.

What you need: Small clean glass bottles or jars; some iodine solution (sometimes called tincture of iodine); a teaspoon; some laundry starch; a selection of foods, including bread, apple, rice, cheese, potato (cooked and uncooked), and milk; a drinking straw or an eyedropper.

What you do: Put a teaspoon of laundry starch in a small jar and cover it with water. Stir the mixture thoroughly. Now, using the drinking straw or eyedropper, put a few drops of iodine solution in the mixture. The mixture will go to a blue-black color. When iodine is added to anything containing starch, this blue-black color is always produced. If something has no starch, the color will not change.

note: Iodine is a poison. Do not let it get near your mouth or eyes. Wash your hands thoroughly when you have finished.

Now get the samples of different foods. Put each sample in a jar or bottle and add a few drops of iodine. Make a table like this to record what you found out:

	Bread	Apple	Rice	Cheese	Potato (raw)	Potato (cooked)	Milk	Meat
color when iodine added	blue-black							
Is there starch ?	yes							

3 Testing foods for fats. Here is another simple food test. When fat touches paper it usually leaves a greasy spot. If the spot is held up to the light, the spot will let light through. Only fats and oils (oils are really liquid fats) do this.

What you need: Some pieces of white paper (paper without lines is best); cooking oil; a selection of other foods that you think might contain fats, including butter, margarine, bread, nuts, potato, orange, cheese, rice, meat.

What you do: First put a drop of water on a piece of paper. Next to it put a spot of cooking oil. Wait for a few seconds. Then hold the paper up to the light. Do you see the kind of spot made by fats and oils?

Now rub the other foods on pieces of paper. Make a table of your results like this:

Food	Makes a greasy spot	Does not make a greasy spot
Cooking oil	✓	
Orange		✓
Butter		
Margarine		
Nuts		
Potato		
Cheese		
Rice		
Meat		
Cabbage		

Which kinds of foods contain fats? Which do not?

4   Can you tell margarine from butter? Advertisements claim that people cannot tell margarine from butter. Is this true? Are the tests used by advertisers fair ones?

What you need: A table knife; slices of bread from the same loaf; butter; margarine; a blindfold; a friend to work with.

What you do: Wash your hands thoroughly before you start the experiment.

Cut the crusts off the slices of bread and cut the slices into equal-sized squares.

Spread some of the squares with butter and some with margarine. Use the same amount of margarine and butter in each case.

Blindfold your friend. Then give him or her one of the squares of bread and butter to eat. Ask him or her what he or she has just eaten. Does your friend get the answers right or wrong? (Remember, that if your friend guesses, he or she is just as likely to be right as he or she is wrong!)

Now give your friend five squares of bread to taste – say three with butter and two with margarine. Can he or she tell you which is which? Is he or she right more often than he or she is wrong? Do you think your friend really can tell margarine from butter? If you change places, can you do any better?

5   Growing mold. Mold is a plant and it grows from tiny particles called spores that float in the air. You can see the dust in the air that contains these spores if you partly draw the curtains on a sunny day. Then look for the little particles floating in the air in the beam of sunlight that comes in the window.

What you need: Some small pieces of food, such as soft bread, cheese, a piece of orange peel, some jam, a little soup, and a little paste made by mixing together flour and water; some clean jam jars; some clean aluminum foil pie dishes; a hand lens or magnifying glass.

What you do: Place one food of each kind in each aluminum foil pie dish. Leave them in a warm place for a few hours and then cover each one with a clean jam jar. Look at the foods every day for several days.

Does any mold grow? Which food grows the most mold? What color is the mold? Where did mold come from?

Look at the mold with a hand lens or magnifying glass. If you can, draw colored pictures of the mold on each food, but *do not touch an*y of them.

How does the mold change as it gets older?

NOTE: When you have finished the experiment, carefully put the food and mold on their aluminum foil dishes into paper or plastic bags. Put them all in the garbage can. If you want to keep the jars, wash them in water to which a little disinfectant has been added.

Wash your hands thoroughly when you have finished.

6 Food colorings. A lot of foods are artificially colored to make them look more attractive. Some cakes are decorated with colored icing, sweets are colored, so are jams and many canned fruits and vegetables. Look on the cans, packets, and jars to see which foods contain coloring. In this experiment we are going to look at some of these food colorings.

What you need: Some strips of white blotting paper or filter paper about 1 inch wide and 8 to 10 inches long; a pencil; a clean jam jar; tape; a drinking straw or eyedropper; small aluminum foil dishes; a selection of colored foods, such as plain

M & M's and Reese's pieces, the green colored water from a can of peas; water.

What you do: First of all put two or three dark brown M & M's in a small jar or dish and add a few drops of water to them. Leave the M & M's in the water to make a dark-brown liquid.

Take one of the strips of filter paper or white blotting paper and, with a pencil, draw a line across, 3/4 of an inch from the bottom.

Put 1/3 of an inch of water in the bottom of the jam jar.

Use the drinking straw or eyedropper to put one drop of the dark-brown liquid from the M & M's in the center of the pencil line on the paper.

Fix the paper onto the pencil with tape and let the paper stand so that the bottom of it just touches the bottom of the jar. Leave the paper in the water for a few hours and watch carefully to see what happens to the brown spot.

What have you learned about the brown color in M & M's?

Now try the experiment with other food colorings.

Let your strips of paper dry and stick them on a large sheet of paper. Label each strip. Display all the strips in your classroom.

Glossary

Here are the meanings of some words that you might have met for the first time in this book.

Bacteria: tiny plants that grow on food and make it decay and go bad. Some kinds of bacteria cause diseases.

Carbohydrates: foods containing a lot of starch and sugar that give us energy.

Carbon dioxide: one of the gases of the air. Green plants use carbon dioxide to help make their food. Fizzy drinks also contain carbon dioxide.

Constipated: when we find it difficult or painful to get rid of the waste food when we go to the bathroom, we are constipated.

Digestion: the breaking up of food into tiny pieces that can pass into the blood.

Digestive system: the long tube and other parts of the body where food is broken down so that it can pass into the blood.

Energy: the go of people, animals, and things. Energy is behind all work and movement.

Fats: foods that give us energy. Fats usually feel greasy and leave a mark on paper that lets light through.

Fiber: the parts of fruits, vegetables, and other plants we eat that cannot be digested.

Food: substances that we eat or drink to help us grow, keep us healthy, give us energy, or keep us warm.

Food chain: a series of animals and plants linked together by their food and what eats them. Food chains always start with plants.

Fuel: anything that will burn and produce energy.

Mineral salts: substances present in all foods that are used in all parts of the body and that help to keep us healthy. Iron and calcium are two kinds of mineral salts that we must have if we are to be healthy and strong.

Mold: tiny plants that grow on food and make it decay and go bad.

Oils: fats that are liquid at ordinary room temperatures.

Proteins: foods that allow us to grow and repair the damaged and worn-out parts of our bodies.

Saliva: the liquid that is added to our food as we chew it. Saliva has a chemical in it that turns some of the starch in food into sugar.

Taste buds: the little red bumps on the tongue with which we taste our food.

Vitamins: substances, named after the letters of the alphabet, that help to keep us healthy. We need only tiny amounts of each vitamin.

Acknowledgments

The publishers would like to thank the following for permission to reproduce transparencies:

G. I. Bernard/OSF: p. 21; British Dental Health Foundation: p. 9 (center) and 22 (center); J. Allan Cash: p. 19 (top left); Bruce Coleman: p. 23 (bottom); Color Library International: p. 20 (top); Electrolux: p. 19 (bottom); Sue Heap: p. 5 (top); Terry Jennings: p. 2, 10, 12, 18 (bottom) and 20 (middle two); Mothercare: p. 8 (top); Oxfam: p. 23 (center); Michael Poulton: p. 5 (bottom left), 6 (bottom), 8 (center), 16, 18 (top and center), 19 (top right), 20 (bottom) and 23 (top); Arthur Shepherd: p. 5 (bottom right), and Syndication International: p. 9 (top).

Illustrations by Joy Barling Loyla, Wendy Brett, Peter Kesteven, Edward McLachlan and Mike Saunders.

Index

1/27/00 ①